Explore
Music
through
Geography

David Wheway and
Shelagh Thomson

19 varied national curriculum
Music activities linked to the
Geography attainment targets

Music Department
OXFORD UNIVERSITY PRESS
Oxford and New York

Oxford University Press, Walton Street, Oxford OX2 6DP, England

Oxford is a trade mark of Oxford University Press

First published 1993
Reprinted 1994
ISBN 0 19 321872 0
Design and illustration by Creative Intelligence, Bristol
Printed in Great Britain by Caligraving Ltd., Thetford, Norfolk

Contents

4   **Introduction**

List of Activities

8   Sounds of Town and Country
9   Weather Chart
10   People at Work
11   Transport
12   Wrap Up!
13   Rainfall
14   Water Music
15   The Seasons
16   Timespan
18   Volcanoes
19   Compass
20   Turtle
21   Weather Round the World
22   What's My Tune?
24   Paper Recycle
25   Inuit Throat Games
26   Rainforest
28   Gamelan
30   Gravel Pit

     Appendix

31   Glossary
32   Pentatonic Scales

There are nine books in this series:

Explore Music through

Art, Geography, History, Maths, Movement,
Poetry and Rhyme, Science, Stories, Word Games.

Introduction

These booklets are designed for primary teachers who value the role of music in an integrated approach to the curriculum. They are of equal value to those who have little or no experience of teaching music, or those who have responsibility as a music co-ordinator.

By closely relating musical activities to other areas of the curriculum, it is hoped that primary teachers will feel more confident when engaging in musical activities with children.

Within each of the nine booklets in the series, activities are ordered progressively from 'early years' through to upper Key Stage 2.

The appropriateness of any activity will depend on the previous experience of the child or group. For this reason we have not recommended any activity for a specific age group, but have indicated a target Key Stage.

Many activities, especially those primarily concerned with composition, are often best delivered over a number of sessions. This allows time for exploratory work, and also for evaluation, discussion, and development.

Building a Repertoire of Sounds

Children need an ever-increasing knowledge of sounds, and teachers need to be aware of the importance of sound exploration for future musical activities. This repertoire of sounds is especially important when children wish to represent feelings, objects, and other sounds in their compositions.

Body and Vocal Sounds

Children should explore the possibility for sounds made both vocally and with the body. For instance, how many sounds can be made with the throat? ('Ooooh', 'Ahhhh', a hiccup, a cough, a gargle, humming, sighing, panting, etc.) What different sounds can be made by patting different parts of the body? (Cheeks, chest, stomach, thighs, knees, etc.)

Classroom Percussion

Children should be encouraged to find as many different ways as possible to play percussion. Can it be scraped, tapped, shaken, scratched, blown, etc.? When a new sound is found, think about what moods or images it conjures up. Such exploration works well in small groups, using a limited number of instruments. Allow the children time to play new sounds to the rest of the class.

Percussion Resources

Some considerations when building resources:

Do your percussion resources offer a wide choice for creating a variety of sounds?

Are the instruments made from a variety of materials (e.g. wood, metal, plastic, etc.)?

Does the collection contain instruments from different ethnic origins?

Are the instruments of good quality? Remember, as in other areas of the curriculum, poor quality materials (e.g. worn or broken) may lead to poor or disappointing results.

Other Sound Makers

A wide variety of sounds can be made with everyday objects such as paper, kitchen utensils, beads and pulses (e.g. paper tearing, scrunching, flapping; pulses poured into a bucket, swirled around, shaken; pots and pans drum-kit).

When performing any activity, try different combinations of sound, as this adds to the children's exploratory work, and their understanding of timbre and texture.

Recording

It is very important that children develop ways of recording their compositions. A variety of ways are suggested throughout the booklets, for example, pictures, symbols, words, letters, and so on. Ensure paper and appropriate recording materials are always available.

Audio as well as video recorders are also valuable resources for recording children's work and development.

The Activities

Suggested Materials

These materials should be useful as a guide for preparing the lessons. They are only suggestions and teachers may wish to select their own materials.

Suggested Listening

Generally, it is a good idea to keep extracts short, e.g. 30–60 seconds in duration. If possible, tape-record extracts beforehand to avoid searching in the lesson.

Most of the suggestions given are easily available in record libraries or through record shops. Many can be found on compilations. Where this is not the case, a reference is given.

The recordings we have recommended should not be considered either obligatory or comprehensive.

Personal collections of recorded music are a valuable resource. However, do avoid limiting the children's listening opportunities to any one type of music.

Attainment Target Boxes

The left-hand box gives an indication of the main focus of each activity, relating to the national curriculum for Music. However it should be noted that the activities will also offer a variety of other musical experiences.

The right-hand box indicates how the activity may complement work undertaken in another area of the curriculum.

Classroom Organization

For many whole-class activities, a circle of children on a carpet or chairs is ideal. This helps concentration and promotes a feeling of involvement, as well as being practical when it comes to observing other children, whole-group involvement, and passing games. It might be advisable at times to split the class or set into groups.

There are some activities that require little or no percussion, and if you are just starting out you may feel more confident attempting these activities initially.

Handing Out Instruments

Avoid the children making a headlong rush to the music trolley at all costs! Allow the children to collect, or hand out, a few instruments at a time.

– Have the required instruments placed out ready beforehand.

– While listening to instructions, children should place their instruments on the floor in front of them.

– Give out beaters for instruments last.

– Before commencing agree on clear signals for stopping and putting instruments down (e.g. a hand in the air, a finger to the lips, a wink of the eye, etc.).

– Demand an immediate response to these signals.

– Encourage children to treat instruments with respect at all times. (This is not easy if instruments are worn or broken.)

Evaluation and Appraisal

When children are working on a composition, there should be regular evaluation by the teacher, and/or by the children, of how the work is progressing. This will include a great deal of purposeful listening and appraising. The process will in turn help the children in appraising the music of others.

Key Questions for Performers and Audience

Can you tell us about your music?

How did the piece start/finish?

What did you like about it?

What contrasts/changes did the piece contain?

Does the piece fulfil the task set?

Was it performed fluently and appropriately?

Could it have been improved, and if so, how?

Could the piece be extended, and if so, how? (e.g. repetition, contrasts, new material, different instruments, etc.)

Did the audience listen well?

The National Curriculum

The boxes at the foot of the page refer to the requirements for the National Curriculum for England, 1992. These have been superseded by the 1995 orders, but the areas of focus for both subjects are still relevant.

Sounds of Town and Country

Suggested Materials

Vocal and body sounds. Instruments and other sound makers.

1. If you are out-of-doors with the children, ask them to be silent for a short while and listen carefully to the sounds around them. If the ground is suitable, let the children lie down and close their eyes.

2. After the children have listened for a while, ask them to say what they heard. Were there any sounds they hadn't noticed before? Were there some sounds they couldn't identify – and if so, can they describe these sounds? Can they distinguish between sounds, and if so, how? Encourage the children to use as many words as possible to describe the sounds (e.g. when asked to distinguish the sound of a lorry from a car, children might say 'Heavier', 'Bigger', 'Lower', 'Slower engine' etc.).

   Children can often work out what a sound is by sharing their descriptions, e.g. 'Tapping', 'Knocking', 'Lots of taps', 'Wooden', 'Echoed', 'Hollow', 'Like a drum' – a woodpecker?

3. Back in the classroom, ask the children to find ways of imitating the sounds with their voices, or using body sounds (e.g. rubbing hands, slapping knees).

4. The children could also try imitating the sounds on instruments, or on other sound makers such as paper or natural materials. Items collected on their walk can be used to create either a similar effect (e.g. dried leaves scrunched to represent someone walking through the leaves), or other sounds (e.g. a fir-cone plucked, or snail shells rattled in a bag – empty ones of course!).

5. The sounds can be used to make up either a short 'sound' story about their walk, or a short sequence of different sounds.

Music Attainment Target: 1 & 2
Main Focus: Listening and Exploring Sounds
Key Stage: 1

Geography Attainment Target: 1
Main Focus: Environment

Weather Chart

Suggested Materials

A few percussion instruments, vocal and body sounds. Daily weather record, e.g. 'The weather today is . . .

1. A common daily activity in an early-years classroom is a discussion/record of the weather. This activity can provide the forum for individual/group improvisation.

2. The weather is often recorded in a pictorial form at this age, e.g.

The weather today is

3. Ask for a volunteer to come and choose a sound source and play some 'windy' music, or 'rainy' music, etc.

4. Value the children's first attempts and then encourage development by asking questions:

– Can you play that again for us?

– Was Paul's music very loud?

– How did Dilip's music start? etc.

Music Attainment Target: 1
Main Focus: Exploring Sounds & Improvisation
Key Stage: 1

Geography Attainment Target: 3
Main Focus: Weather

People at Work

Suggested Materials

Access to a variety of percussion. Vocal sounds and junk material.

1. Discuss with the children the different roles of adults they see regularly, e.g.

   a) Who brings the milk/post?
   b) Who sees them across the road?
   c) Who looks after them in their home?
   d) Who empties the bins?

2. Choose a few of these roles to use in a sound trail. Discuss sounds to go with the trail, e.g.

   a) footsteps, bottles clanging, footsteps.
      footsteps, letters dropping on mat, dog barking, footsteps.
   b) sounds of traffic, traffic slowing and stopping, footsteps, traffic moving off again.
   c) making a cup of tea (filling kettle, putting out cups, kettle boiling, pouring water into teapot, pouring tea into cups).
   d) rubbish lorry arrives, footsteps, clanging gate, dragging bags across ground, machine churning rubbish, rubbish lorry departs.

3. Along with the children, find ways of representing these sounds, vocally, on percussion, and on junk material (e.g. eggboxes, yoghurt cartons).

4. Place the events in an order, and aim for a fluent change from one scene to the next. A picture score may help (see activity **'Water Music'**).

Music Attainment Target: 1 & 2 Main Focus: Exploring Sounds Key Stage: 1	Geography Attainment Target: 4 Main Focus: People at Work

Transport

Suggested Materials

Body and vocal sounds initially, percussion and other sound makers later on.

1. Ask the children how many different ways they can think of to make a journey. Can they find vocal and body sounds to represent these different forms of transport?

2. Once they have explored the possibilities for sound, decide on an order and use these sounds to create a trail. The children make their sounds in the appropriate place(s).

3. Link all the parts of the trail together with one repeated mode of transport, e.g. walking.

Extension Activities

1. Can the children find other sounds (sound makers/percussion) to represent the different modes of transport? (Try experimenting with different sounds in small groups over a period of time.)

2. Repeat the trail, incorporating the new sounds with the body and vocal sounds used earlier.

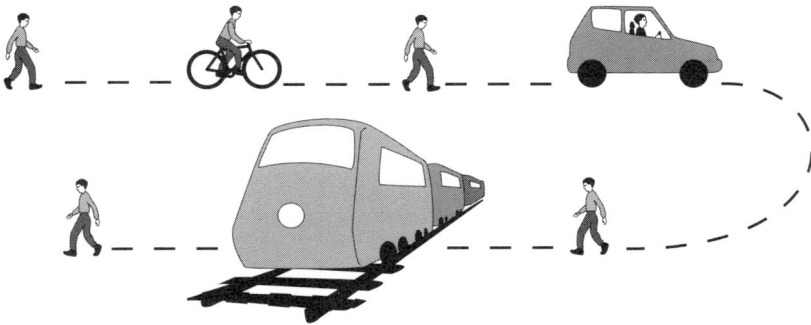

Music Attainment Target: 1 & 2	Geography Attainment Target: 4
Main Focus: Exploring and Composing	Main Focus: Ways of Making a Journey
Key Stage: 1/2	

Wrap up!

Suggested Materials

Vocal sounds.

1. Discuss with the children how the wind can make many different sounds:

   The wind...
   whistling through the doorway;
   howling down the chimney;
   rustling through the leaves;
   sighing, humming, crying, etc.

2. Can the children find appropriate vocal sounds for these examples? What other words can they find to describe the wind? What other vocal sounds can they discover that sound like the wind?

3. The class sit in a circle. Divide the circle of children into groups. Each group has one sound. A child is chosen to be the conductor. S/he stands in the centre of the circle and points to groups, who start their sound. The conductor raises his/her hand to stop them. Sometimes only one group will be making their sound, at other times lots or all of the groups will be joining in. Discuss the results with the children.

Music Attainment Target: 1	Geography Attainment Target: 3
Main Focus: Composing	Main Focus: Weather
Key Stage: 1/2	

Rainfall

Suggested Materials

An assortment of percussion and sound makers.

1. Ask the children if they have noticed how rainwater makes different sounds as it lands on different surfaces. Make a list of different surfaces (e.g. pavement, car roof, shed roof, window, tent). Find words to describe the differences (e.g. 'splashy', 'tinny', 'soft', 'splattering', 'thudding', etc.).

2. Now using an assortment of instruments and beaters, the children find which sounds most closely resemble these descriptions, e.g.

   Xylophone (soft beaters) – pond, puddles
   Tambour (drumming fingers) – shed roof
   Maracas (shake fast) – window
   Tambour (pour in dried pulses) – pavement
   Tambour and swirling beans – car roof.

3. Use the sounds to create a piece about the rain.

Music Attainment Target: 1	Geography Attainment Target: 3
Main Focus: Exploring and Composing	Main Focus: Forms of Water
Key Stage: 1/2	

Water Music

Suggested Materials

See suggestions below.

1. Discuss with the children what forms water can have. Think about how these different forms can be represented in sound, e.g.

   Water dripping (woodblock, tulip block, tongue clucking, light clapping).

   Crunching through snow (paper crunching, guiro scraping).

   Pitter patter of raindrops (squelchy mouth sounds, patting knees, finger clicking).

   Still pond (gentle taps on chime bars, triangle, Indian bells).

   Heavy rain (slap knees fast, dried peas swirling in tambour or large tin, beads poured into waste-paper basket).

   Steam (hissing mouth sounds, shaking maracas, scraped skin of tambour).

   Gently flowing river (ascending and descending notes on a xylophone).

2. These sounds could be ordered, using the pictures, to create the children's own 'Water Music'. Duplicates of the pictures could be used to encourage repetition.

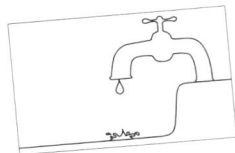

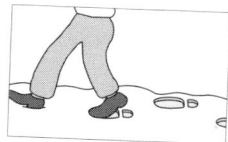

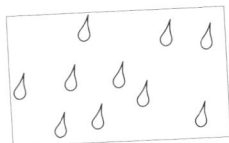

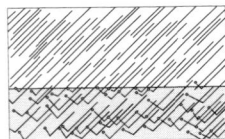

Music Attainment Target: 1 Main Focus: Composing Key Stage: 1/2	Geography Attainment Target: 3 Main Focus: Water

The Seasons

Suggested Materials

Access to a variety of percussion, body and vocal sounds.

Suggested Listening

Adagio from 'Autumn' and the opening to 'Spring' from *The Four Seasons* by Vivaldi, 4th Movement from Beethoven's Symphony No. 6.

1. Think about what colours are associated with each season, e.g.

    Winter – blue, grey, white

    Spring – green, yellow

    Summer – orange, blue, yellow

    Autumn – brown, gold, orange.

    Can the children think of sounds to go with these colours?

2. Discuss what other things are associated with each season, e.g.

    Winter – icicles, snow, bare trees, hibernation

    Spring – pollination, showers, growth

    Summer – hot sun, thick foliage, tall grass, flies

    Autumn – falling leaves, harvesting.

    Find sounds to represent these things.

3. Combine sounds together in a seasonal sequence.

Music Attainment Target: 1 & 2
Main Focus: Composing
Key Stage: 1/2

Geography Attainment Target: 3
Main Focus: Seasons

Timespan

Suggested Materials

Posters, pictures, or children's own art work, showing the 'development' of an area over a period of time (see opposite). Class percussion and other sound makers. (Audio tape-recorder for extension activities.)

1. Talk about the nature of a real or imagined place, and what it might have looked like in the past (see first picture).

Find sounds to go with different parts of the picture (e.g. ducks on the pond, the labourer ploughing, the mill wheel turning). Order these sounds into a short piece of music (or sequence of sounds).

2. Consider what changes would have occurred over the next 100 years. Find appropriate sounds for the additions to the picture (e.g. mining, transport, communications). Incorporate these sounds into the original piece, and omit sounds that are no longer appropriate.

3. Repeat the above process until the final picture is up to date. Discuss both the resulting music and the changing scene with the children.

Extension Activities

Tape record the resulting pieces to stimulate further discussion, and to assist evaluation.

| Music Attainment Target: 1 |
| Main Focus: Composing |
| Key Stage: 2 |

| Geography Attainment Target: 5 |
| Main Focus: Environment |

1790

Farmer ploughing
Church
Graveyard
Farmhouse
Duck on pond
Mill
Stream

1890

Traction Engine
Men on way
    to work
Church
Graveyard
Workmen's
    cottages
Farmhouse
Mill
Stream
Steam Engine
Pit/Slag heap

1990

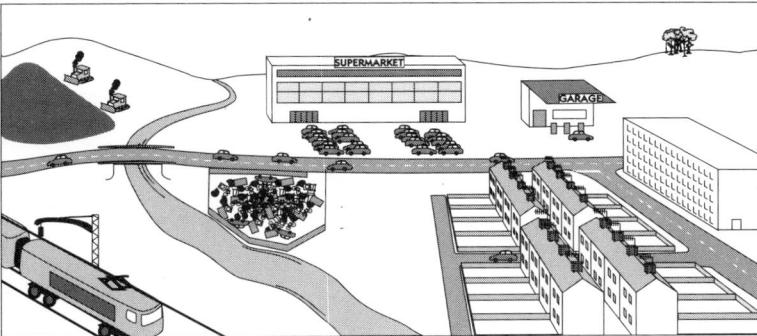

Offices
Garage
Supermarket
Cars
Estate - TV aerial
Dump
Electric train
Bulldozers

Volcanoes

Suggested Materials

Percussion and sound makers. Picture or video of a volcano (erupting if possible).

1. Discuss the nature of a volcano, and make a list of possible sounds that would be useful for volcano music, e.g.

> Molten rock under pressure – stretching creaking sounds, door creaking, guiro scraped.
>
> Rip/crack in earth – thunderclap, paper/card being torn
>
> Gas and steam escaping – hissing mouth sounds, circular scratching on drum skin, paper crumpled, maracas shaken.
>
> Lava erupts – thunderclap, keyboard sounds, crashing cymbals, castanets rattled, wobble boards
>
> Dust settles – wind chimes, chime bars, sandpaper rubbed together.

2. Organize the children into groups with responsibility for the different sounds. Discuss how these are to be combined to illustrate the eruption of a volcano.

Extension Activities

If you have a video of a volcano erupting, turn the volume down, and use the children's ideas to produce a soundtrack.

Music Attainment Target: 1
Main Focus: Composing
Key Stage: 2

Geography Attainment Target: 3
Main Focus: Volcanoes

Compass

Suggested Materials

Four instruments which can be easily distinguished from one another (e.g. woodblock, tambourine, bells and cymbal). Compass.

1. Discuss compass points with the children, emphasizing that North and South are opposite to each other, as are East and West. Using a compass, establish the direction of North with the children. Now ask the children to find a space and face North.

2. On hearing the sound of one instrument, they take one step forward.

3. Now select another sound. On hearing this, the children take one step backwards (South).

4. Now play a series of sounds on the two instruments, the children responding appropriately after each sound.

5. Once all the children can do this successfully, introduce two more sounds for one step left (West), and one step right (East).

Extension Activities

Increase the difficulty of this activity, by choosing sounds which are more closely related (e.g. woodblock, claves, tulip block and wooden agogo).

Use different rhythms for the directions based on the first line of well-known songs, e.g.

North – Frère Jacques
South – This Old Man
East – Pease Pudding Hot
West – Land of the Silver Birch.

Music Attainment Target: 2
Main Focus: Listening
Key Stage: 1/2

Geography Attainment Target: 1
Main Focus: Directions

Turtle

Suggested Materials

Four instruments which can be easily distinguished from one another (e.g. woodblock, tambourine, bells, and cymbal).

1. 'Turtle' is similar to 'Compass' in that it uses sounds to indicate which movements the children should make. In this game the children move forward and back but instead of stepping sideways, they turn through 90 degrees to left or right depending on the sound.

2. Set up a short maze in the hall. Can the children direct a blindfolded child through the maze using their sounds?

Extension Activities

This activity could be extended with the children responding to four different melodies played on chime bars, e.g.

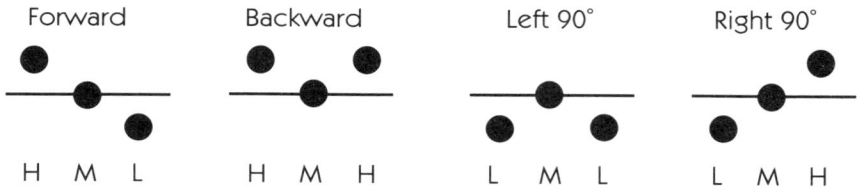

Forward	Backward	Left 90°	Right 90°

H M L   H M H   L M L   L M H

Groups of children might like to make up their own melodies for this activity and record them as above.

Music Attainment Target: 2	Geography Attainment Target:1
Main Focus: Listening	Main Focus: Directions
Key Stage: 2	

Weather Round the World

Suggested Materials

Access to a variety of percussion. Map C in the Geography national curriculum folder.

Suggested Listening

Recordings of music associated with weather, e.g. *The Four Seasons* by Vivaldi, *Alpine Symphony* by Richard Strauss (extract from 'Thunder and Storm'), extract from the 4th movement of Symphony No.6 by Beethoven, extract from the 'Hebrides' Overture by Mendelssohn, 'Troika' from the 'Lieutenant Kijé' Suite by Prokofiev, opening of *The Desert Music* by Steve Reich (CD 7559-79101-2), extract from *La Mer* by Debussy.

1. Discuss weather conditions in different parts of the world. Look at three contrasting regions and ring these on the world map, e.g.

> Greenland = cold conditions in polar regions
> Australia (outback) = hot, dry conditions in tropical deserts
> Malaysia = hot, wet conditions in tropical forests.

2. The children then decide on sounds to represent each region, e.g.

> A = random notes on white and black chime bars, Indian bells, vocal wind sounds, crunching paper
> B = cymbal, rhythmic maracas, guiro scraped
> C = vocal tropical bird sounds, swirling maracas, occasional gentle slap on legs for rain.

3. Arrange the sounds for each region into a short piece.

4. Going on a circular route from Britain, visit each region, then return home. Decide on a motif to represent travelling, e.g. short rhythm or melody.

Music Attainment Target: 1 & 2 Main Focus: Composing Key Stage: 2	Geography Attainment Target: 2 & 3 Main Focus: Weather

What's My Tune?

Suggested Materials

Grid chart (see next page), plus three chime bars: a high, a medium, and a low pitch (i.e. a short, medium, and long respectively). Reproduce copies of the chart for group work. This activity can be introduced to the whole class. Once it is understood, the children could work together in groups.

1. One child decides on a tune (e.g. low – high – medium) and gives the appropriate grid reference (4a). A second child plays the appropriate tune. If it is agreed s/he has played the correct tune, then the children swap.

2. To make a longer tune give two or three references. (It may be a good idea if these are close together vertically or horizontally – e.g. 4a, 4b, and 4c.)

Extension Activities

The child with the chime bars plays a tune, and the second child has to find the tune and give its reference. This activity could be played like the game 'Battleships', with tunes being marked off the grid when correctly identified.

Music Attainment Target: 2
Main Focus: Listening
Key Stage: 2

Geography Attainment Target: 1
Main Focus: Co-ordinates

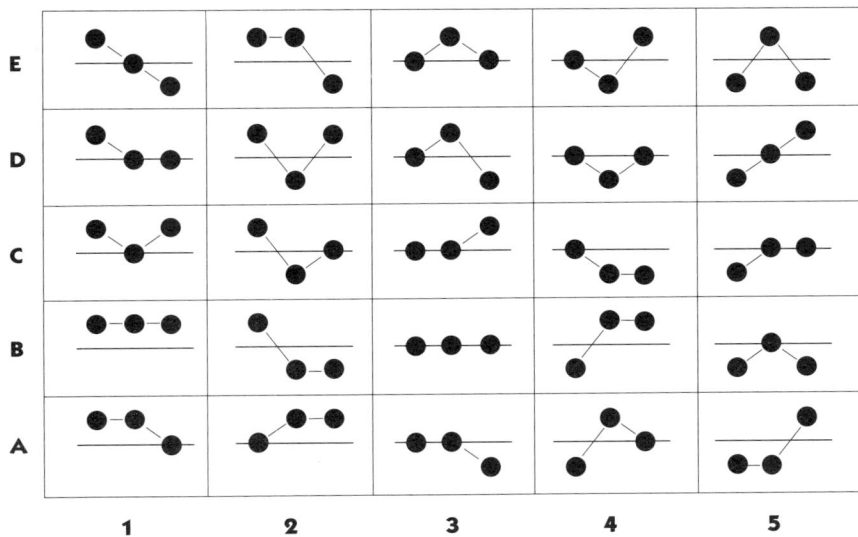

This is quite a large grid. At first it might be preferable to use a smaller grid, i.e. with fewer tunes (1-3, A-C).

Paper Recycle

Suggested Materials

Vocal sounds. An assortment of different types of paper. A series of pictures or a written list showing the following sequence in order.

1. A person reading a newspaper
2. Paper being pushed into a recycling bin
3. A lorry transporting waste paper
4. Paper being mashed at the processing plant
5. Paper being produced on rollers

1. Explore the possibility for making sounds with different types of paper, e.g. rolled, crumpled, flicked, waved, blown, rubbed.

2. Use these sounds to represent the various stages of paper recycling. Add vocal sounds where appropriate (e.g. hum of lorry, squelching sounds for paper mash).

3. The children could make a sequence of their paper sounds, e.g. Paper: flicked – crumpled – flicked – rustled – flicked – crumpled – flicked.

Music Attainment Target: 1 Main Focus: Composing Key Stage: 2	Geography Attainment Target: 5 Main Focus: Environment

Inuit Throat Games

Suggested Listening

Recordings of Inuit throat games. If you have difficulty, ask at your local record library. One CD available with lots of different examples is *Canada - Jeux vocaux des Inuits* (Ocora/Radio France co-produced with Faculté de musique de l'université de Montréal – C559071), also Inuit Games and Songs (Philips *Musical Sources* 6586036).

Inuits have numerous vocal games, often played with a partner. Two people stand facing each other with their hands on each other's shoulders, and sometimes crouching.

Vocal sounds are made in a variety of ways: sometimes words, sometimes panting, sometimes syllabic.

Sounds are often repeated in a rhythmic way, partners making the same sounds, or different sounds.

The example below is of a type of throat game where the partners make their sounds in turn, creating interesting rhythms and sounds.

Ask the children to invent some throat sounds (they may have some unusual sounds already), or think of words that they could use to create their own game. Using words of more than one syllable juxtaposed with their partner's single-syllable words can set up interesting rhythms, e.g.

happy   happy   happy

     sad   sad

Give emphasis to the word happy by panting on the 'h'. The children stand face to face with their hands on each other's shoulders. Who can keep the game going the longest without losing the rhythm, or giggling?

Music Attainment Target: 1 & 2 Main Focus: Exploring Voices Key Stage: 2	Geography Attainment Target: 2 Main Focus: Knowledge & Understanding of Places

Rainforest

Suggested Materials

Xylophones, swannee, and other whistles (including vocal).

Suggested listening

Music by Nana Vasconcelos; the music for the film *The Mission; Forêts De L'Amazone/Forests of the Amazon*, Pierre Huguet-Olivier Tostain (CD Sittelle 1990).

1. Set up a rhythm layer as below. Start by counting aloud from one to eight several times, then ask the children to follow the first line only on the chart, clapping on the circled number while still counting aloud one to eight. Practise one line at a time, repeating the line until the children have achieved an acceptable degree of accuracy.

(1)	2	3	4	(5)	6	7	8
1	(2)	3	4	5	6	(7)	8
(1)	2	3	(4)	5	6	7	8
1	2	(3)	4	5	6	(7)	8
1	2	(3)	4	5	6	7	(8)

2. Once the children can do this successsfully, divide into groups to clap two or more lines simultaneously. Decide before beginning how many times you are going to repeat the lines. Remember to practise slowly at first.

3. Experiment with instrumental and vocal sounds to create sounds of the rainforest (e.g. birds, dripping water, rustling leaves, monkeys, hissing, etc.).

4. Divide the children into groups and use the rhythm layer again, this time making the sounds of the rainforest on the circled numbers, e.g.

hiss	2	3	4	hiss	6	7	8
1	drip	3	4	5	6	drip	8
whistle	2	3	whistle	5	6	7	8
1	2	rustle	4	5	6	rustle	8
1	2	whoop	4	5	6	7	whoop

Extension Activities

The layers could be used to represent the natural layers of a rainforest, with bird sounds at the top, on the first line, and insect sounds on the lowest line, with leaves, humans, and animals in between.

Music Attainment Target: 1 & 2
Main Focus: Rhythm and Composing
Key Stage: 2

Geography Attainment Target: 5
Main Focus: Environment

Gamelan

Suggested Materials

A variety of percussion using the pentatonic scale (see Glossary), e.g. glockenspiels, chime bars, metallophones, xylophones (including bass xylophones/metallophones if available).

Suggested Listening

Recording of gamelan music.

'Gamelan' is the native music of Indonesia and although complex it is possible to produce a simplified type of gamelan with primary children.

1. Ask a few children to spend some time practising the short melody below.

    (r = rest and is therefore silent)

1	2	3	4	5	6	7	8
C	D	E	(r)	A	G	E	(r)

    The children practise the melody until they can play it over and over, steadily, and together.

2. Those on higher-pitched instruments play the melody through repetitively, while the children on lower-pitched instruments play the notes of the same melody in sequence, one on every fourth beat. It is important to work slowly at first, and neither part should forget any rests. Example:

    ($G1$) C-D-E-(r)-A-G-E-(r)-C-D-E-(r)-A-G-E-(r)-C-D-E-(r)-A-G-E-(r)-C-D-E-(r)

    ($G2$) C   D   E   (r)   A   G   E   (r)

    ($G1$ = group 1, $G2$ = group 2)

3. If the children can hold this together they might like to try adding a third group, who play through the sequence, joining in on every fourth note of Group 2. It requires patience and very careful counting to hold the piece together, and children should avoid speeding up, or else the whole thing will collapse.

4. Now encourage the children to invent their own simple four-beat melodies. (NB Advise the children to avoid complicated melodies, as this makes the activity much more difficult.)

Extension Activities

A further group might like to improvise pentatonic melodies above the ostinato layers of the other children.

Music Attainment Target: 1 & 2 Main Focus: Rhythm & Composing Key Stage: 2	Geography Attainment Target: 2 Main Focus: Knowledge & Understanding of Places

Gravel Pit

Suggested Materials

Vocal sounds. Access to a variety of percussion.

1. Display the following pictures, and discuss what is happening in each.

2. Discuss the possibilities for composing music to match the pictures:

A – birds singing, flowers and trees growing, wind through the trees.

B – diggers, conveyor-belt, engine sounds.

C – As A above.

Suggestions for sounds:

Birds singing (vocal whistling, Indian bells and chime bars).

Plants growing (notes on xylophone played from low pitch to high. Swannee whistle(s)).

Wind through trees (puffing, blowing vocal sounds).

Diggers (rhythmic tapping and shaking on percussion).

Conveyor-belt (vocal hum).

Engine sounds (vocal rhythmic sounds, representing engine sounds e.g. 'Chugga chugga...', 'Oompa, oompa...', 'Dum! – Dum!'):

Extension Activities

These pictures can be used as a starting point for discussions with the children about the importance of looking after the countryside, e.g. – Why do we have gravel pits? Is it a good idea to return the land to its former condition after extraction of minerals?

Music Attainment Target: 1 Main Focus: Composing Key Stage: 2	Geography Attainment Target: 5 Main Focus: Environmental Change

Appendix

Glossary

Crescendo   Getting louder.

Decrescendo   Getting quieter.

Drone   One or more notes maintained throughout a piece.

Dynamics   The gradations of volume in music.

Form   The order in which different ideas appear in a piece of music.

Improvisation   Composing spontaneously while performing.

Glissando   The process of moving from one note to another quickly, while playing all other notes in between.

Notation   The symbolic written representation of sound(s).

Ostinato   A rhythm or melody pattern repeated regularly during a piece of music (often as accompaniment).

Pitch   The perception of sounds as 'high' or 'low' in relation to each other. A woman's voice is usually higher in pitch than a man's.

Pulse   A repetitive, regular beat (sometimes silent), which can indicate the speed of a piece of music.

Rest   'Musical silence' – the absence of a sounding note or notes.

Rhythm   The pattern which long and short sounds and rests make when heard in sequence.

Rhythmic independence   The ability to maintain a rhythm against other rhythms.

Score   A written record of all the parts in a piece of music.

Sequencing   The ordering of sounds.

Timbre   The characteristics/colour of sound(s).

Volume   The loudness or quietness of sound/music.

Symbols

f Loud

p Quiet

$<$ Getting louder

$>$ Getting quieter

Pentatonic Scales

The notes on tuned percussion should be arranged with long bars to the left, getting increasingly smaller to the right-hand side, and in alphabetical order. Most (but not all) start with 'C'.

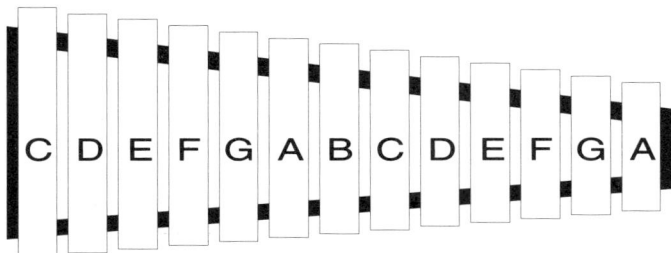

By removing any note 'B' and any note 'F', it is possible to have a five-note scale, called 'Pentatonic' (Penta = five). This should leave a sequence of C D E G A.

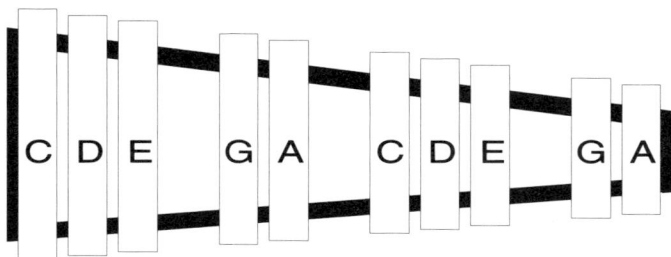

A pentatonic scale is useful for improvising melodies, both solo and in group work.

Occasionally instruments will come with notes called 'sharps' (with a ♯ after the letter), and 'flats' (with a ♭ after the letter), e.g. C♯ E♭ F♯ G♯ B♭ By using only these notes, it is again possible to create a pentatonic scale. This same scale can be found by just using the black notes on a piano or keyboard. Use this scale if most of the notes on your tuned percussion are sharps and flats.